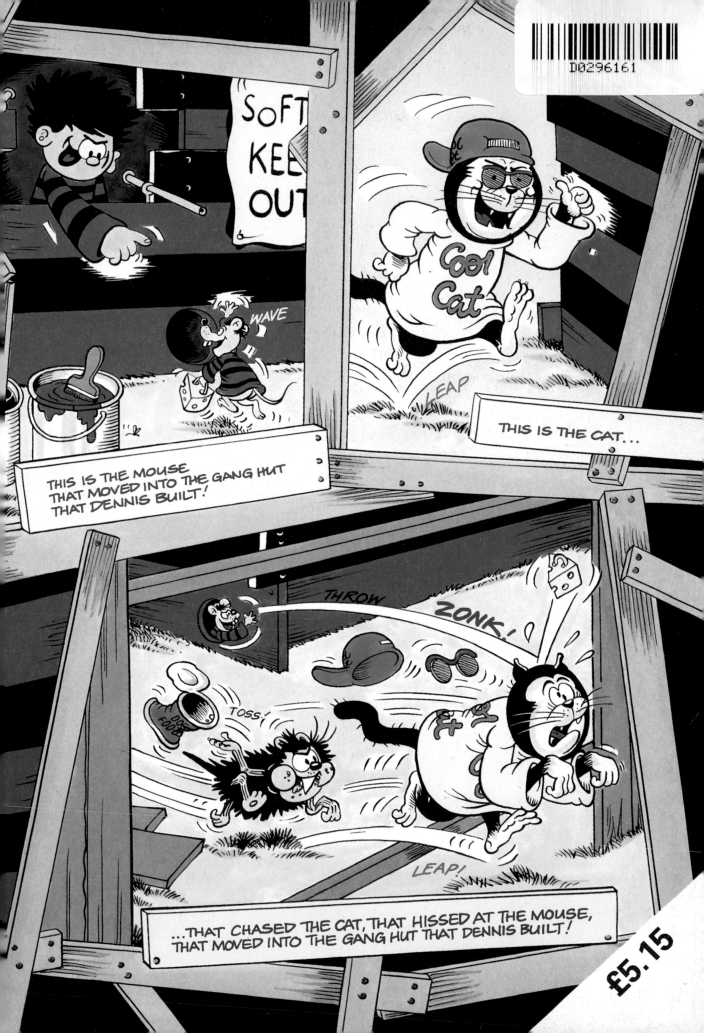

Printed and Published in Great Britain by D. C. Thomson & Co. Ltd., 185 Fleet Street, London EC4A 2HS. © D. C. Thomson & Co., Ltd., 1998.

ISBN 0-85116-667-9

WATCH OUT

HAW! HAW!

DENNIS IS AT THE FOUNTAIN!

THIS IS THE ONLY WAY I CAN KEEP UP WITH HIM!

PLAN OF 'BEANOTOWN'

HERE'S OUR HELICOPTER ROAD REPORT...

IDEA

HAR-HAR!

ROTTEN EGGS

WE'RE HAVING A LOVELY TEA PARTY— AREN'T WE?

WHIRRR!

THROW

SPLAT!

BLAST OF AIR

YUGH! WHAT A TIME FOR A GALE TO SPRING UP!

TEE-HEE!

BAH! THE WIND WAS FROM THAT HELICOPTER!

BLAST!

DENNIS TRAFFIC WATCH

BODY LANGUAGE

WE'LL NOW SHOW YOU THE "C" FOR CURLY SIGN!

WHIRR

THROW

SWISH!

EEK!

SWASH!

SPLOOSH!

SWISH!

THAT'S HOW EASY IT IS, READERS!

A HUMAN BOOMERANG!

BACK IN THE GARDEN·

HERE'S ANOTHER SIGN, DENNIS...

EH?

"D" FOR DAD!

BOOOMF!

ERK!

HEH·HEH!

SNAP

SNAP

HEY! DAD'S GETTING INTO THE SPIRIT OF THE THING!

CLAP

WHO'S DOING THAT?

ERK! IT WAS "M" FOR MAD MUM!

DIRTY MY WASHING, WOULD YOU?

BANDANARAMA!

LOTS OF TOUGH GUYS WEAR THOSE HEAD BANDS!

"RUMBLE"

GNESH!

I NEED MY SUBSTITUTE JERSEY HERE!

ONE FOR ME, AND ONE FOR GNASHER!

RIP!

NOW WE LOOK TOUGHER THAN EVER!

GNASHEE!

WHAT GOOD ARE THESE THINGS? HEE! HEE!

I'LL SHOW YOU!

ROTTEN APPLE

PLUCK

WATCH!

HAW-HAW!

THEY'RE NOT ONLY FOR DECORATION!

SPLUTCH!

OOYAH! MUMSIE! HELP!

CLAP!

MIND YOUR MANNERS

IT IS GOOD MANNERS TO USE CUTLERY AT ALL TIMES.

IT IS GOOD MANNERS TO USE FINGER BOWLS AFTER A MEAL.

SNOW JOKE

WIG-WHAM-BLAM!

So—

RED AND BLACK, BIG POCKETS, TOUGH MATERIAL AND SEND THE BILL TO DAD!

TAILOR-MADE ANORAKS

Soon—

AND NOW FOR SOME MENACING WITH THE ANORAK!

YOU'VE NO SNOWBALLS! TEE! HEE! I CAN THROW SNOWFLAKES AT YOU!

SOFTY WALTER BEING VERY BRAVE

FOO-FOO, PAMPERED PUP

NO SNOWBALLS, EH?

WHAT D'YOU CALL THIS, THEN?

WHUMP!

FEELING BRAVE BECAUSE GNASHER'S NOT ABOUT, EH?

YAP! YAP!

UNZIP

WAH!

THIS MENACEORAK IS A GREAT THING!

GNASH!

SQUASH

At home—

MMM! IT LOOKS LOVELY AND WARM!

GLAD YOU LIKE IT, DAD...

...HERE'S THE BILL!

EEK!

BILL TO DAD ONE SPECIAL ANORAK £150

WE'LL HAVE TO TAKE IT BACK!

HUH!

NO CHARGE—EVERYBODY'S WANTING MENACEORAKS!

PHEW! THAT'S A GOOD THING!

R-I-P!

£150

BUT I COULD BE WRONG—GROAN!

GREAT POCKETS, EH?

SPLAT!

THROW

...EQUALS... BUMP!

...ONE MENACE LEFT ON THE ICE! HAR-HAR!

OOER!

Soon—

GASP! MORE SOFTIES!

YOU LIFT ME SO DIVINELY, DARLING!

YEEK! AND SO HIGH!

LIFT

YAARGH!

LIFT

SHRIEK!

TOPPLE

SLAP

HOW DARE YOU DROP ME!

CACKLE!

I'M SURE YOU'LL BE A MUCH BETTER PARTNER!

EH?

TRA-LA-LA!

SPIN

W-W-WOW!

DIZZY SPIN

WOBBLE

THAT'S NOT VERY ELEGANT!

I'LL HAVE TO FIND ANOTHER PARTNER!

DAZED

GNERK!

MOAN! REMIND ME TO STICK TO MENACING BEARS AND COMMANDOS—ICE DANCERS ARE TOO DANGEROUS!

WE GIVE YOU GAS!

Dear Dennis's dad,

For the past few years Beanotown Gas Board Inspectors have been trying to read your gas meter, but every time we sent one, they would come back with their uniform and nerves in tatters! We have discovered that the answer lies with your two dogs — Gnasher and Gnipper.

We have tried to send gas bills through the mail, but the poor postie never seems to be able to deliver them without having his uniform and nerves left in tatters too! This is why this letter has been dropped down your chimney by helicopter.

You now owe £799.99 to Beanotown Gas Board. Please pay without delay.

Yours faithfully,

M. E. Thane

M.E. Thane.

A FANTASTIC STORY

I'M TIRED OF SEEING DENNIS AND WALTER IN THE SAME OLD STREET. GIVE ME SOME SWORDS AND SORCERY THIS WEEK!

BEANO EDITOR

"EVERYONE WE KNOW READS THE "BEANO"

YESSIR!

In another time lived Prince Walter The Soft...

His main foe was Lord Dennis The Menace.

YOU ARE POWERLESS BEFORE THE SWORD OF FLOWERINESS!

NICE SCENT

I TOLD YOU! I AM TRIUMPHANT!

FLOWERY NIFF

DON'T BE SO SURE, SOFTY!

GNASH! GNASH!

TITTER!

LEAP

WASH and GO!

DINNER!

THUNDER OF BACON

SPLUTCH!

CHOMP!

Much guzzling later—

NO NEED TO CLEAN RASHER'S TROUGH AFTER HE'S EATEN...

SHINING CLEAN

...BUT THERE'S PLENTY OF NEED TO CLEAN RASHER.

OINK!

Soon—

I KNOW HOW TO GET IT DONE, THOUGH.

FLIP!

FLOP!

LET'S GO FOR A RIDE IN MY NEW CAR...

GREAT!

...TO THE CAR-WASH!

OINKWAH! TRICKED.

VAROOOM!

CAR WASH

CAR WASH CONTROL

BRRRM!

NEXT, PLEASE!

But—

WHIRR!

PHUT!

CAR WASH CONTROL

I'M NOT WASHING THAT FILTHY THING —OUT!

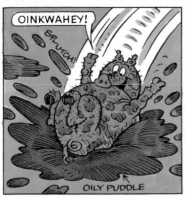

OINKWAHEY!

SPLUTCH!

OILY PUDDLE

AT LEAST ONE GOOD THING WILL COME OF ALL THIS...

BRRRMM!

...MY PLANTS WILL GET AN EXTRA WATERING.

SWOOSH!

HOW OFF-PUTTING

DAFT PSYCHOLOGIST

SCREAM!

SPLAT!

SOOT BOMB

SOOT BOMB

THAT POOR LAD IN THE STRIPED JERSEY NEEDS HELP TO STOP HIM BEING NAUGHTY.

AVERSION THERAPY

Later—

THIS'LL BE A LAUGH!

TIP TOE

HERE GOES!

SHOVE

9+7
−3+
2 =

SCRATCH GRIND

9+7
−3+
2 =

OOH! ARGH! THE PAIN!

HEH! HEH!

YURGH!

THRUST

OOH! WHAT A LOVELY DAY TODAY.

WHAT A TOPPER

At school—

SOFT LITTLE WALTER

BLEH!

FANCY PENCIL TOPPER

WALTER'S LUNCH BOX

SUCH A LOVELY PENCIL TOPPER!

YEUCH! I FEEL ILL!

FRAGRANT AROMA

WALTER'S LUNCH BOX

HUH! MUST FIND A MENACING PENCIL TOPPER!

THIS'LL DO!

PROD

SNIFF! SNIFF!

HEY! THAT'S MY TOMATO!

HAVE IT BACK THEN!

SPLUTCH!

TWANG!

LOTS OF FUN TO BE HAD WITH PENCIL TOPPERS!

GOING DOWN the DRAIN

WONDER WHERE WE'LL POP UP NEXT?

RING-A-RING O' ROSES!

SPIN

SOFTIES

ZOOM!

ALL FALL DOWN!

WAH!

SOON—

NO SIGN OF THAT NASTY GNASHER!

TOPPLE

EEK!

HAR-HAR!

GNAR! GNAR!

URGH!

SPLOORGE!

Meanwhile—

OOO! I'M SO EXCITED!

POUR

ONE OF MY GREATEST EVER INVENTIONS!

SWEET SMELL

TO WALTER'S GARDEN

LET'S POP UP AND MENACE THE SOFTY!

THIS SHOULD MAKE OUR TOWN'S DRAINS SMELL SWEETLY—OOPS! I'VE POURED IT ON THE MENACES!

POUR

HUH! IMAGINE SPENDING A DAY IN THE SEWERS AND ENDING UP SMELLING LIKE THIS! GROAN!

GIGGLE!

SWEET SMELL

HEH-HEH!

LOVELY PONG

TALL TALE

THERE'S NO-ONE ABOUT TO MENACE — SO I'LL TELL YOU A TALE OF LONG AGO.

GNBAH!

TALES OF LONG AGO

THUMP!

Young Lord Dennis is menacing Prince Walter of Softness!

PUSH

EEK!

LORD DENNIS'S DAD'S GARDEN

VENUS SOFTY-TRAP FLOWERS

SUDDENLY—

HEY! WHAT'S GOING ON?

GRAB

SNAP.

EEK!

DINNER!

THAT'S IT, GNASHER!

GIANT GNASH!

HAW-HAW! TICKLES!

ERK!

JURASSIC LARK

In class— NOW FOR THAT HISTORY LESSON I PROMISED YESTERDAY!

YAHOO!

OH, NO!

READER → I DON'T BELIEVE THIS—DENNIS LIKING HISTORY!

YAH!

PREHISTORIC MONSTERS TYRANNOSAURUS REX

TUG

IT'S A LESSON ON DINOSAURS!

WAH! EEK!

I **DO** BELIEVE IT NOW! ←READER

DESIGN WHAT YOU'D HAVE LOOKED LIKE IF **YOU** WERE A DINOSAUR!

BEST DAY AT SCHOOL EVER!

CLAP! CLAP!

HOW'S THAT?

A MENACEAUR

HAIR AFFAIR

TIME FOR ANOTHER STORY ABOUT LORD DENNIS THE MENACE IN ANOTHER TIME!

WHAT A LOVELY BLOOM!

I HAVE TO PUT UP WITH THIS ALL THE TIME!

TUG

GASP! THAT FLOWER'S MADE A DOOR OPEN!

WHAT'S INSIDE?

AARGH! IT'S HORRIBLE...

GNORRIBLE!

WELCOME!

AARGH! IT'S THE HALL OF THE MOUNTAIN SOFTY!

FLOWERY PERFUMY SMELL!

NICE NIFF

GNBAH!

HEY! WHAT'S HAPPENING?

OPENING TRAP DOOR

A PASSION for FASHION!

MIND YOUR MANNERS

IT IS GOOD MANNERS TO EAT FROM A METAL PLATTER.

IT IS BAD MANNERS TO SPEAK OR GRUNT WITH YOUR MOUTH FULL.

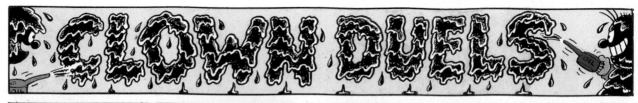

DUELLING WAS A COMMON FORM OF SETTLING ARGUMENTS IN THE NINETEENTH CENTURY!

WHIRR!

WONDER IF THAT HAS GIVEN DENNIS ANY IDEAS?

CLICK!

OH, Y-YES IT H-HAS!

At home~

CAN'T FIND A GLOVE TO SLAP ANYONE'S FACE WITH, THIS SOCK WILL DO!

PUNGENT PONG

GNWAH!

IT'S A DUEL!

WHIFF! PONG!

THWACK!

RIGHT! GUNS AT TEN PACES!

FIRE!

OIL

WHERE'S MY OIL GUN?—DENNIS!

OIL

'BYE, DAD!

GRAB

SLIP

FOR THAT, I CHALLENGE YOU TO A DUEL!

BUMP!

PIE-FACE

PIES

HE CHOSE PIES AT FIVE YARDS!

FLUMP!

BLURP! YOU WIN, DENNIS. GREAT! HIC!

PHEW! THAT WAS HARD WORK!

Then—

I CHALLENGE YOU TO A DUEL, DENNITH!

THIS ISN'T LIKE LES.

LISPING LESTER

PUNTHETHS AT FIVE YARDTH!

OKTH!

SWISH!

GIGANTIC SWISH!

HAR! HAR! DON'T NEED TO BE NEAR YOU!

SHOCK WAVES

BUMP!

MY TURN TO CHALLENGE YOU TO A DUEL!

HAR! HAR! DON'T MAKE ME LAUGH!

PANSIES AT NO YARDS!

CRUSH

ULP! FAINT!

In Menace ward~

PILL DISPENSERS

DUELS— HUH!

PHUT!

PILLS

LAVA STORY

IS DENNIS GOING TO HELP HIS DAD IN THE GARDEN?

YOU MUST BE JOKING!

SQOON—

EVERY MENACE'S GARDEN SHOULD HAVE A VOLCANO!

PAT

A VOLCANO—HOW FASCINATING! I'VE BEEN READING ABOUT THEM IN GEOGRAPHY LESSONS!

SOFT LITTLE WALTER

OOER! IT'S GOING TO ERUPT!

SHUDDER

A MENACING ERUPTION!

FAINT

EEK! AM I BEING CARRIED ALONG ON A TIDE OF LAVA?

FLOAT

NO, YOU'RE BEING CARRIED ALONG BY US, YOU SOPPY WEED!

SOB!

COMPOST HEAP

HEH-HEH! LOOK WHERE THE "LAVA FLOW" LEFT HIM!

CHINESE RESTAURANT

THIS IS TOO HOT FOR HUMAN CONSUMPTION!

FIZZ!

HEAT

STOP, I CAN FIND "SUMPTION" TO DO WITH IT!

SO—

IN SHE GOES!

POUR

BURBLE!

THERE SHE BLOWS!

FIZZ!

FIZZ!

KABOOM!

WHAT AN ERUPTION!

SPLAT!

SPLAT!

SPLAT!

SPLAT!

SPLAT!

SPLAT!

THEN—

HE'S MADE HIS OWN VOLCANO, HAS HE?

MUMFLE!

YOU NEVER STOP, DO YOU? ALWAYS MENACING, ALWAYS ANNOYING NICE PEOPLE...

...YOU'RE BANNED FROM WATCHING TV, POCKET MONEY STOPPED FOR EIGHT YEARS, AND GNASHER'S GETTING FISH FLAVOURED DOG MEAT, AND, AND, AND...

ERUPT

SHAKE

WOW! WHO NEEDS A VOLCANO WHEN YOU'VE GOT AN ERUPTING DAD?

SUBSIDE

IMPRESSED

DENNIS THE MENACE
THE FASTEST CARTIE IN THE WEST

And they galloped through the market square,
Den's fan club badges on his chest.
His name is Dennis and he drives,
The Fastest Cartie In The West . . .

Now Dennis has an enemy,
Who likes to howl and squeal.
Called Walter, Prince of Softies,
And he drives the Scent Mobile . . .

He tempts customers with his bubble-bath,
And his scented perfume sprays.
And the slightest whiff of his after-shave,
Could knock you out for days . . .

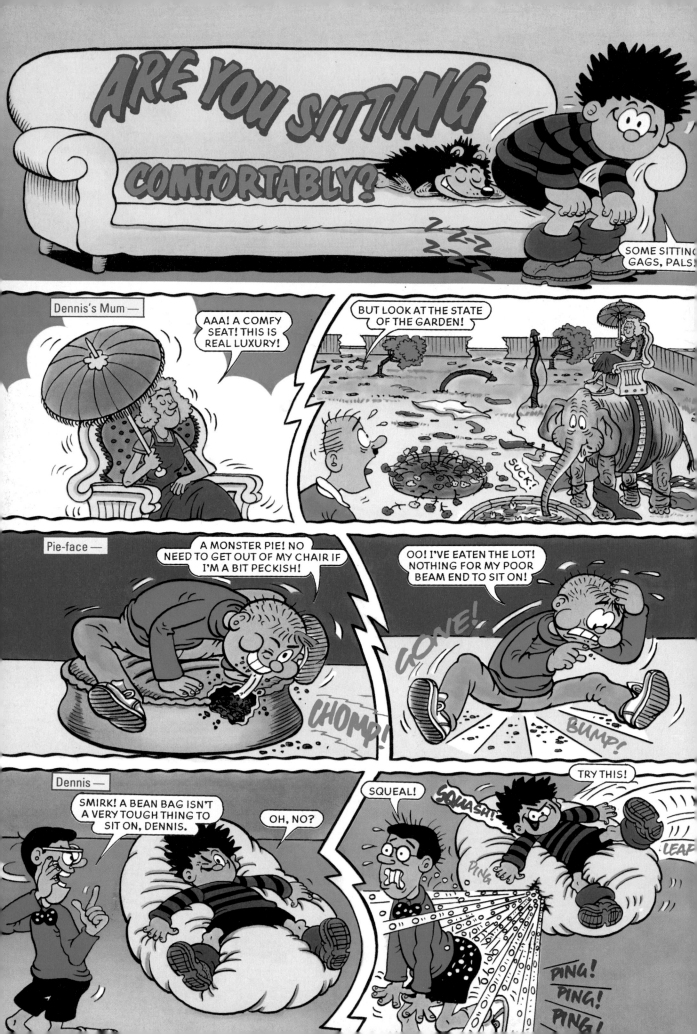

EEK!

TRUNDLE

GASP! IT LOOKS HUMAN—COULD BE A MAN FRIDAY!

WRONG! IT'S MENACE EVERYDAY!

HOWL!

SHAKE

TREMBLE

OOH! IT'S LIKE AN EARTHQUAKE!

TOUGH! IT'S PLASTIC AND YOU CAN'T EVEN EAT IT!

CATCH

SCREAM! A GREAT WHITE SHARK!

SWOOSH!

WRONG! IT'S A LITTLE BLACK DOG!

BOO! HOO! MY ISLAND PARADISE IS TURNING OUT ALL WRONG!

SHAKE

AHOY, FELLOW MENACES!

But—

AAHOOHOOHA!

ERK!

I'M NOT WORRIED ABOUT THIS BIG, NASTY WORLD OUT HERE ANYMORE...

SKIP

GRR! WAIT TILL I GET MY HANDS ON YOU!

CLIMB

OOER!

GNEEK!

WAH!

...ALL THE NASTY, MENACING THINGS HAVE MOVED TO MY ISLAND!

Later—
I'M GOING TO BE SOMETHING MORE MENACING THAN A FLY!

DAD'S OLD RUGBY JERSEY

OW! WOW!
WAH!
TWANG!
HEH! HEH! A WASP'S GOT A BIT MORE STING! AND THESE ANTS EGGS HELP!

TIME FOR ANOTHER CHANGE!
STING OINTMENT

SPRAY
SPRAY
BLUE
MUM'S OLD RUG
NET CURTAIN

WAAH!
BLOW
BLOW
BLOW
BELLOWS

I'M DENNIS THE SPIDER NOW!
I'M STUCK!
BLAST
BELLOWS
EH?

STUCK
WE'LL SAVE YOU FROM HIS CLUTCHES, SWEET BUTTERFLY!
BELLOWS

SCREAM!
GNASPSH! GNASPSH!
IT'S A GNASHERPILLAR!

HELP! SAVE US FROM THAT HORRIBLE MONSTER!
GNASPSH!
THAT DOES IT— I'M OFF TO THE 'BEANO' PRINTING WORKS!

Then—
OOH! IT'S GONE DARK!
RIGHT! —YOU LITTLE INSECT!

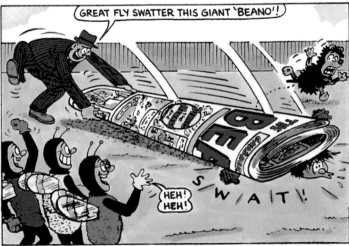
GREAT FLY SWATTER THIS GIANT 'BEANO'!
HEH! HEH!
S W/A|T!

IT'S NOT FAIR

BAH!

WIN A TEDDY

SURELY PEOPLE DON'T LIKE SOFT PLACES LIKE THAT FAIR!

Back home—

I'LL GIVE THEM SOMETHING BETTER!

BANG! BANG!

MENACELAND 50p ENTRY

DO WE GET A TICKET?

NO—I'LL KNOW YOU'VE PAID WHEN GNASHER DOES THAT!

RIP!

A WELCOMING FIGHT TO START WITH!

THUMP!

THUD!

FRUIT HOOT

OO! WE LOVE SOFT FRUIT!

PICK YOUR OWN FRUIT & VEG.

HOLD ON, YOU!

NOW I'LL REMEMBER THAT WEIGHT!

ONE FOR THE BASKET, ONE FOR THE TUM!

NNNG... CAN'T GET THIS BERRY!

ONE FOR THE BASKET— SEVENTEEN FOR MY TUM!

HOI! YOU LOT!

SNIP!

SQUELCH!

MIND YOUR MANNERS

IT IS BAD MANNERS TO SCRATCH AT THE TABLE.

SCRATCH

SCRATCH

BOING!

LEAP!

BOING!

S

P

IT IS BAD MANNERS TO READ AT THE TABLE...

...BUT WHO CARES?

GNASHER

THE BEANO

THE GANG HUT
that Dennis built

TOSS! ZONK! LEAP!

THIS IS THE SOFTY, THAT RAN FROM THE D[...] THAT REWARDED THE [...]

THIS IS THE DOG THAT REWARDED THE PUP, THAT CHASED THE CAT, THAT HISSED AT THE MOUSE, THAT MOVED INTO THE GANG HUT THAT DENNIS BUILT!

DELICIOUS CHEESE 'TOASTIE' AROMA

GANG HUT

THIS IS THE GRANNY, THAT MADE THE CHEESE TOASTIE, THAT TRIPPED THE SOFTY, THAT RAN FROM THE DOG, THAT REWARDED THE PUP, THAT HISSED AT THE MOUSE, THAT CHASED THE CAT, THAT MOVED INTO THE GANG HUT THAT DENNIS BUILT!

SLURP!

THUNDE[...] OF TROTTER[...]

THIS IS THE PORKER, THAT SNIFFED GRANNY'S CHEESE TO[...] THAT TRIPPED UP THE SOFTY, THAT RAN FROM THE DOG, THAT REWARDED THE PUP,